BICYCLE COWBOY
AND OTHER POEMS ABOUT GROWING UP

To Mark

Ron Helmboldt

BICYCLE COWBOY

AND OTHER POEMS ABOUT GROWING UP

RON HELMBOLDT

Parkhurst Brothers Publishers

MARION, MICHIGAN

www.parkhurstbrothers.com

Parkhurst Brothers books are distributed to the trade through the Chicago Distribution Center, and may be ordered through Ingram Book Company, Baker & Taylor, Follett Library Resources and other book industry wholesalers. To order from Chicago Distribution Center, phone 1-800-621-2736 or send a fax to 800-621-8476. Copies of this and other Parkhurst Brothers Inc., Publishers titles are available to organizations and corporations for purchase in quantity by contacting Special Sales Department at our home office location, listed on our web site. Manuscript submission guidelines for this publishing company are available at our web site.

Printed in the United States of America

First Edition, 2016

2016   2017   2018   2019   2020   12 11 10 9 8 7 6 5 4 3 2 1

ISBN: Trade Paperback   978-1-62491-089-0

Parkhurst Brothers Publishers believes that the free and open exchange of ideas is essential for the maintenance of our freedoms. We support the First Amendment to the United States Constitution and encourage all citizens to study all sides of public policy questions, making up their own minds. Closed minds cost a society dearly.

Cover and interior design by: Linda D. Parkhurst, Ph.D.

Proofread by: Bill and Barbara Paddack

Acquired for Parkhurst Brothers Inc., Publishers by: Ted Parkhurst

112016

DEDICATION

*This collection is dedicated to all the people, young and old,
that were a part of my life growing up in Marion, Michigan.
That would include most of the entire community
during the 1950's and 1960's.*

ACKNOWLEDGMENTS

I was inspired to try writing in free verse because of the work of my cousin, Terry Wooten. Then Jim Lithen created a literary marvel, The Marion Millennium, which gave me a printed outlet. Without these two it just wouldn't have happened. And then there is the typing and editing by my wife, Cathy, and son, Andy. Thanks.

CONTENTS

PREFACE

When I grew up during the 1950's and early 1960's in Marion, Michigan was a time of freedom and independence for a kid. The town in north central Michigan was small, friendly, busy, and a virtual playground in which to roam. If the tallest structure in the village wasn't a tree, it had to be the water tower or the grain mill. Farm families came to town every Saturday evening (before television), and the old men sat on wooden benches along Main Street while their wives shopped at one of three small groceries, the Ben Franklin Store, or Rosie's dress shop. I developed a knack for experiencing and telling stories during this time which is the background for my poetry.

After graduating from Central Michigan University, I became a career high school teacher and coach in Sparta. In the fall, I coached football, in the winter, wrestling, and in the spring, baseball. My wife, Cathy, sons, Andy and Joe, my students and athletes all endured stories of life "back in the day" in Marion.

Stories always seemed to be flowing at family gatherings and especially in Fred and Mel's Barber Shop. Fred was my paternal grandfather and Mel was my dad, so the acorn didn't fall far from the tree. So you are invited to sit back and indulge. And ride along with the Bicycle Cowboy as he pedals down life's road.

PART 1
TRYING TO GROW UP IN
MARION, MICHIGAN

Introduction

Marion is a small, rural town in north-central Michigan near Cadillac. The poems (free verse) in this section tell stories about childhood, adolescence, and high school memories. I grew up in a pleasant atmosphere where one was free to just be a kid. The following poems are close to chronological order. The first one, "The Rookie," took place when I was in kindergarten. The girl is now a retired elementary teacher in her seventies, living in Greenville.

In one of our many conversations about our past adventures, Jim Lithen nailed it precisely, "The whole town was our playground." The freedom each kid enjoyed to ride his bicycle anywhere in town or to nearby farms, seems an illusion today. In those days, before modern media and the parental anxiety it has engendered, we kids spent every daylight hour making up games, playing any kind of ball sport, or investigating the frogs and crayfish of the pond or river. The wide variety of activity growing up in this environment was wonderful.

I. The Rookie

They walked hand in hand
out the back of the school
"want to see my bear?"
he wanted to impress her
"you have a real bear?"
She was taken aback!

The story grew bolder
block by block
into something amazing
"Yes, a bear and all sorts
of other wild animals."
He was on a roll
she wanted to see
what lurked in the dark
shed behind his house.

He grew uneasy nearing
his appointment with truth
wondering how his Angus calf
could be turned into
a black bear how
two fat rabbits and
a blind duck would
serve as wild animals.

She giggled her way
home telling everyone to
beware of the big bear
up at Helmboldt's.

He never lived down
that first big one

but being a kindergartner
meant more stories were
destined to flow from
the lips of this rookie.

II. Old Lady With A Hoe

Her overgrown lot shaded
all but a room sized plot
yielding tomatoes, beans, beets, squash
gingerly coaxed from dirt
seemingly too thin.

She seemed too frail to
work the soil or pump water
but every summer day her
tiny shawl-draped body shuffled
around the plot scratching an
incredibly ancient hoe
cutting out weeds and stones
gently sprinkling thirsty plants.

Becoming acquainted took time
visiting briefly while cutting
cross lots to the ball field
her voice a faint, hoarse whisper
trying to temporarily break
spells of elderly loneliness
listening to jabbering adolescence
just to postpone monotony.

Her house dark and musty
sent willies down my spine
feeling haunted old spirits

watching me looking at
pictures, utensils, tools, furniture
seemingly from another century
but in everyday use here.

Forty years later visions
come back. Sometimes while
weeding my garden, I can
hear her hoe scratching,
see that frail frame hunched
over her sprinkle can
shocking me to reality,
realizing I am now
closer to being the
Old Lady With A Hoe
than the young visitor.

III. Coloring Eggs

1930's Great Depression's grip
didn't allow for simple frills
like Easter egg coloring kits
leaving Park Lake ridge runners
improvising home remedies.

Trial 'n error found things
that worked making Great-Grandma
Helmboldt the resident expert
showing grandkids 'n neighbors
how to color Easter eggs.

Big tea kettle steaming
hot on the wood stove,
ready to mix vinegar,

boiling hot water with
colors brought up from
the root cellar.

Canned goods in particular
brought impressively colored
reds from beets 'n raspberries,
yellows from peaches 'n squash,
deep huckleberry purple;
things that stained your shirt
colored eggs well too.

Most remarkable was onion skins
boiled in vinegar water
dipping eggs in timed intervals
produced golden, then orange and
finally a deep bronze-toned
egg never seen anywhere else.

As kids, we shunned this
old-fashioned gibberish as
archaic nonsense when handy
professional looking coloring kits
sat waiting on the dime
store shelf not realizing
tradition-rich homestyle coloring
had it all over watery
cheap store-bought stuff.

IV. Bicycle Cowboy

Apaches lurked in Lewis' pines
zipping arrows 'n blood-curdling screams
hoping to catch greenhorns
coasting too slow.

Sioux and Cheyenne roamed open
spaces along Johnson's alley
speedy ponies seeking chases
bringing sure death to unswift
ones unable to escape.

Wooded tangles behind Grandma Brown's
protected painted Pawnee 'n Blackfoot
hunting scalps collecting wampum
trading chips spent gleefully
at the Middle Branch penny store.

One traveled constantly alert
armed to the teeth
revolvers-carbine-skinnin' knife
gear strapped on tight
ready for flight or fight.

Some days speed alone
saved yer bacon
pumping Blackie hard sending
lead while dodging trouble.

Other days Blackie lay
hidden in weeds waiting out
forays into bushes, corn patches,
orchards, tall grass often surrounded
pinned down for hours.

Blackie the Schwinn never
let me down never
left me stranded never
allowed savage or beast
take us for torture
or death.

A more loyal steed
never cruised Marion trails
asking so little
giving so much time
so many thrilling escapes
so many magic moments
for a bicycle cowboy.

V. The Great Spark Plug War

It started over Francis McCann
shooting at Jeanne's cat
trying out his new
Red Ryder air rifle.

Howling cat couldn't drown
screaming insults hurled
over the split rail fence
catching me in the middle
paint brush flapping wondering
was it Tom or Huck tricked
those kids into white washing
his back fence?

Robert Frost's poem
"Good Fences Make Good Neighbors"
was shot full of BB holes

as a boiling brouhaha caused
sides to form for battle
testing neighborhood loyalties confirming
who's mad at whom
at that particular time.

Opposing forces formed quickly
eight or ten per side
mounting Schwinns and PF Flyers
like mighty war steeds
racing down sixth street
brandishing stick weapons designed
to jam into spokes
launch green apple bombs
fling dried cow chips
spraying brown shrapnel.

Pouncing on Doug Kipp's gunny
sack of used spark plugs
stashed at Archie's Junkyard
our gang pelted 'em raining
rusty fouled plugs off
charging foes while shielded
behind the old Creamery walls.

My best throw caught
Jeanne cheek-side slicing a
boxer-like cut sending blood
running down her neck,
stopping all fighting cold
causing me to rush up
just as she whirled
air mailing a fist-sized rock
special delivery
upside my head.

Just like that!

War over -- gangs dissolved
two sweating bleeding combatants
hobbled home to mothers
wanting to know "the story."

No one was supposed to
get hurt or stitches either
apologies were made
gang warfare on Marion's
NE side fizzled as
peaceful tranquility returned.

And I got the fence painted.

Author's Note: The next two, "Kibby's Field" and "Inkster Colored Panthers"
illustrate what role baseball played in my life.

Our playing field was a block-sized vacant lot owned by Revoe and Emily Ida Kibby.
It was all grass, had a chicken wire backstop, burlap bases, Hartzog's garden (in play)
in deep right, a homemade high jump and pole vault pit in left.

The Colored Panthers were my favorite touring team. They were good, fun, exotic, and
a startling contrast to our lifestyle.

VI. Kibby's Field

Modern Major League players
show little love for the game
drawing the ire of the old timers
who lived just to play
choosing The Game over less
worthy pursuits leaving more
casual activities --- swimming,

biking, fishing, reading comics,
drinking Kool-Aid to non-players.
My big black Schwinn Racer
cruised daily Jim Greengrass glove
draped over handlebars holding a
brown Mel Ott 33 in. Louisville Slugger
seeking a game---500, work-up
anything using a baseball.
Sometimes Karl Wilson and I
went one-on-one home run
or out all afternoon.

Real games meant choosing sides
family-street-neighborhood rivalries
fought and replayed hundreds of times
ultimate matches being against
guys from west of M-66 coming
to challenge our turf --
Kibby's Field.

Wooden bats mostly Louisville's
Al Kaline, Hank Aaron, Nellie Fox
models bought at Morton's Hardware
or gleaned broken from

Marion Independent games had to
be glued, screwed, and taped.

Lessons learned-shared-passed
down to younger lads
flexible rules changing
guys came and went
reducing the field size
no leading off
pitchers hand was out.

You played all positions

batters had to catch
umpires nonexistent creating
great arguments--no fights.

Occasionally dads stopped by
needing a little fix
being an all-time pitcher
staying young saying
"I should do this more often!"

Kibby's Field lasted the '50's
thru our childhood
ending with urban sprawl
new houses, driveways, garages
kids shoved off to
organized Little League ball
adults ordering them around
handing out t-shirts 'n caps
taking life out of the game
kids never knowing baseball
when it was King.

VII. Inkster Colored Panthers

Baseball created special memories
players coming into Marion
battling our fabled Independents
known to knock down
storied teams like GR's
Sullivan's Furniture or
Flint Kelly Homes
crushing lesser nines
daring to risk reputation
at Veterans Park.

About 1955 or '56 black
Detroit hardballers called
Inkster Colored Panthers
drove long Cadillacs north
crashing our 7th of August
celebration bringing blaring
bluesy music painted
ladies swinging pearls
singing songs never
played on WATT, Cadillac.

Being bat boy gave me
unobstructed views to
barnstorming action far surpassing
NBC Game of the Week.

Chasing errant throws
fouls into woods 'n weeds
filling water jugs
kept my butt hoppin'
still able to hear
rich stories flowing
like Red Man juice
tales of bygone games
flowed while men swigged
Coca-Cola and Dr. Enuf.

Marion infield practice meant
being alert to hot-wired
catcher Jumpin' Jack Fewless
foggin' throws to bases
making "take one 'n cover"
more warning than order.

Panthers' infield practice
combined dancing feet with
loud jive-talking chants

rifle arms smacking
ball to leather in rhythm.

Two innings remain clear
forty years after crouching
near on-deck hitters watching
crazy-Jack baseball unfold.

First inning -- no score
runner on -- two out
big first-sacker clean-up hitter
came striding smiling twirling
a cannon-sized Louisville Slugger
fingers long enough to wrap
twice around the handle
digging in showing teeth
big as piano keys.

Jack leaped up waving
his catcher's mitt directly
behind the Panther's
ear screaming "put her
right here, Mel."

Sure enough fastball
smoked high 'n tight
chin music sending the big
Panther flying backward Jack
screaming "Atta Boy, Mel."
"Hum Baby"
"Shoot the Mitt"
Three times running
Jack's glove waved
behind his ear
three high hard ones
popped the ragged mitt.

"Crazy mother" shrieked the
fallen first sacker
howling thru swirling dust
slapped from pants 'n shirt.

Next pitch zoomed in
fastball down the pipe
frozen Panther unable
to swing as Jumpin' Jack
shot outta his crouch
spearing the ball while
landing on the plate
screaming "oooh-ahhhh"
firing the ole pea
back at the mound.

Second pitch rode in
sweetly grooved again
Jack springing out
snapping it straddle
the plate grunting ooh-ahhs
while Umpire Robinson
rang up "steeee-rike two."
strike three came in
leaving the big Panther shell shocked.

As classic battles often do
we rolled into the ninth
game on the line
tied 2-2. Jack
leading off hitting
style clearly defined
"two for the crowd,
one for Jack."

Bat twice too big
whirling around lifting

Jack 'copter-like spinning
complete 360 hat flying
shirttail flapping missing
by a mile -- strike one.

Anyone not catching
all this magnificent motion
could catch the instant replay
as strike two sailed
in amid the flourish.

Take this to the bank --
Jack would hit
whatever came next
usually 'bout cap high
both spikes rising
bat whirling wildly
eyes glued on the ball
crack -- single to center.

Number two hitter
Stan methodically "Roped"
his patented "take two'
hit to right"
setting the table where
Big Mel often dined.

A belly tight heater
brushed him back
he tightened the grip
set the jaw hard
ready for the hook
launching it high 'n deep
crash landing in the maple
beyond left field
....ball game!

Send those city
boys home.

VIII. Warehousing

Old Ann Arbor RR warehouse
stood boarded shut leaning uneasy
tight between the alley trail
and tracks along the river
unused 'cept to hold old depot junk
providing housing for RR ghosts
needing quiet moments to reflect
on days when RRs were King.

Once busy with hissing engines
stopping for coal and water
pushing north to Frankfort
waiting to ride the big
ferry boats to Wisconsin
now quiet home to spiders
bats, mice, spirits lurking
behind signs warning all
to stay away from here.

Most kids figured the place
haunted keeping a fair distance
while cutting through RR alley
on runs to Middle Branch Grocery
called the penny store by
every kid in town.

A few dared exploration
conquering fear crawling up
thru rotting floorboards into

spooky darkness clearing
dust-clogged cobwebs clinging eerily
to ball caps sticking to fingers
searching out safe boards
to tread on in the stale air.

Ghosts can be elusive
choosing to perch in far
corners watching every breath
chuckling at constant nervous chatter
meant to hold them at bay
knowing one boooo would
scare hair straight --
times like this made
me hum and whistle
"Casey Jones" hoping
spooks here would dig
RR tunes reminding 'em
when they danced holdover
Saturday nites at Copemish Legion Hall.

Like mean dogs, ghosts
eventually allow comfort zones
recognizing our boldness
awarding respectful passage
like one of the family
accepting four of us to
make regular visits but
not to wear out our welcome.

Hiding bikes in tall weeds
crawling in Saturday mornings
while other kids watched
Buster Brown ads on TV
we hid listening for girls
chattering down the alley
innocently heading for penny candy

to be jolted by invisible
ghosts sending chilling howls
out boarded up windows
sent screaming girls racing
down RR alley charging
into the Penny Store gasping
urging something be done
about the horrible ghosts
in that ugly old building.

Don't remember when the
old warehouse came down or
RR alley got paved but the
ghosts all left in 1959
moving up the tracks
to Park Lake hanging out
around the old tool factory ruins
still talking about days
back in Marion when guys
could have a little fun.

IX. Spikehorn

John - Jack - Grizzly Ike
Spikehorn or just plain Spike
part frontiersman - part shyster
carefully cultivated image drawing
travelers to his bear den
penned deer, coons, black bears fed
by hand from nickel dispensers.

No neutral character, he:
love him or hate him
be charmed or be stiffed

countless forays into court
Harrison, Clare, Mt. Pleasant, Shepherd
fights over land, unpaid bills, taxes
brought pages of free publicity
like the time he brought
Bruno into Legislative Chambers
in downtown Lansing endearing
his character to fans.

Mom never liked it there
disgusting smelly bear pit
flies buzzing bear dung piles
Spikehorn competing with bears
for most odiferous in camp.

Dad didn't love it either
cheap Indian 'n frontier trinkets
bored him to indifference
but Spike's long greasy hair
left his barber fingers twitching
wanting a shot at that
tangled yellow-gray mane.

Kids - at least boys - loved
feeding bears, petting deer, scratching
raccoon rumps watching Bruno
nibble candy from Spikehorn's
lips like a big baby.

Took city-bred cousins there
to suck in country smells
swat some flies shuck peanuts
chucking them at bears rearing
up on haunches posing
for cameras to shoot them.

Aunt Lorna has a picture

proving I descended
into the bear pit putting
an arm around Blackie
showing off to downstate cousins
a story to be retold
a hundred times making me
part of Spikehorn legend.

Spikehorn's Bear Den grew
as US-27 traffic thickened
the 1950's lifestyle seemed to
match this attraction until
Spike died in '59 ending
an era rich with lore
pioneer days blending with
motorized tourists mixing past
lifestyles of log cabin and buckskins
to weekend up north tourists.

Spikehorn's place rapidly crumbled
weeds and spiders claiming niches
ignoring passers-by wondering
what happened to the animals?

What became of regular
two lane highways where
people stopped now 'n then?
what happens to change
our interests making such
places backward and obsolete?
My cousin and I drove
over there one Saturday
sat by the creek wondering
if we could ever fall
for a place like that
in the 60's laughing
at what passed for real

entertainment in those days.

X. Swimmin' Hole

Hot summer days once
broken up by bus rides
to Rose Lake Park
now could be relieved
in our own Swimmin' Hole.

Remember the day well
construction started by blocking
dam flow allowing barefoot
kids free reign chasing
fish trapped in receding pools
Sible's Hardware sold out
every bullfrog spear and
trout net in stock.

Chamber - Kiwanis - Rod 'n Gun
Club men came nightly
hand mixing cement piling rocks
throwing dirt creating the Hole
walled on two sides
huge diving plank deeply
anchored into an earthen bank
rubber shower mat nailed
over the rough edge
protecting tender feet ready
to spring skyward.

Kids flocked daily
killing summer heat
dipping in frigid flowing

river water cold enough
to frost your nugies
on 80 degree days.

Lifeguards changed now and then
Coach Dietz, Johnie Isenhart, Eugene Baughan,
Ted Fewless stood watch
whistling rowdies even allowing
me an occasional turn.
Crazy things happened some days
creativity went bonkers like
Dale Alberts riding our bikes
across the dam spillway
or off the diving board
monster tractor tube wars
turning into dunk fests
diving contest interesting
in that no-one actually
knew how but allowing
uninhibited original creations
flopping 'n splashing wildly
variations of Cannonballs
proved most popular.

One 7th of August celebration
we raced to wall 'n back
first place - 50 cents, second a quarter
girls modeled swimsuits like
little Miss Marions hoping
to win a blue or red ribbon
causing hot rivalries
fueled by zealous moms.

Carefree days spent there
captured the essence of summer
free to swim - read comics
listen to Betsy's transistor radio

pulling in WKNX in Saginaw
turning lazy afternoons into
time well spent.

Evenings were a mixed bag
farm boys rinsing hayseeds
older guys with day jobs
joining to crank off
some dives before cruising
Cadillac's Hillcrest Drive-in
leaving the Hole for Pike
fishermen like me 'n Denny Alberts
he smashing his minnows
leaving blood scent to
lure big toothy monsters.

Heart gripping moments came
worst ever being the day
we left the water while
older guys dived until
our friend Benny was found
taken from us forever.

Another startling one came
when a leisurely morning
casting spinners turned
into horror when "Doc Junior"
snagged the young downstate boy
who'd fallen in a half-hour earlier.
Bob never fished the
Swimmin' Hole again but has
saved several kids since.

The Swimmin' Hole kept
working its summer magic
giving kids a place
a chance and time to

meet and be friends.

XI. Hauling Hay

Some guys did the loyal routine
same fields, equipment, style
familiarity bred confidence
acting like they owned the place.

Others freelanced bouncing around
anywhere bales popped out
meeting farmers on the street
variety spiced trips to the new farm
destinations - Winterfield, Highland, Vogel Center,
learning different ways listening
to equipment debates bragging
on John Deere, Farmall, Alles-Chalmers.

Townies gained valuable new skills
driving tractor, stacking bales, riding conveyors
walking barn beams, chasing cows, AND
the ultimate trick...persuading
rookies to pee on
an electric fence.

Some farmers were valued for
great lunches and $1 an hour wages
others were ducked avoiding
baloney sandwiches and warm Kool-Aid
some had hot new machinery
others barely out of the Depression.

Honest sweaty, dusty, hot work
brought that special glow

riding the last load in
stacking the barn stashing
hard cash in jean pockets
enough to buy your way
into the Sun Theatre
ice cold Coca-Cola
warm popcorn
a ride to Cadillac
burger 'n fries, chocolate malt
it didn't get any better than that.

XII. Eagle Football

We started young
watching heroes stroll
out a side gym door
lacing up hightop spikes
modeling over-sized smelly
leather helmets practicing
maroon gladiator moves.

Legends jogged casually
daily migrating to practice
clicking metal on cement
dodging cars snaking along
winding trails to Veterans Park.

Bryce Swiler, Jack Baker, Fred Sible,
imposing manboys laughing
teasing runt grade schoolers
following on bikes cutting up
Turner's yard slipping behind Bontekoe's
timing their trip to match
Coach Deitz's arrival.

Game nights meant struggling
to see thru tree-like men
wearing huntin' coats
rubber boots caked with
blended mud 'n barn residue
leaving few gaps for
peering thru hoping to
catch game action flowing
up and down the sideline.

Did see Ron Meis
seemingly sockless leaping
jam piles for yardage.

Saw the Lee family
scurrying out kit in hand
reattaching Mose's wooden leg.
Saw Ernie Richardson muddy
playing trumpet at halftime
scampering for the bus
catching last second instructions.

Saw Fred Thompson high step
crashing the line could never
tell when he had the ball.

Finally got to H.S. in 1959
lined up for equipment
freshmen dead last
Leon Mosher, Dan Williams, and I
received the last maskless
leather helmets and OLD blue shirts
ever worn at MHS
prompting humorous reference
later in my Senior Echoes.

Equipment budgets being small

frosh served as blocking-tackling
crash dummies for varsity's
bigger meaner stronger horses
earning us sideline seats
every Friday night riding
rocking busses to enemy turf
Harrison, Lake City, Coleman, Evart,
watching Bill Kibby run right
run left run back kicks
and keep on ticking.

A new coach arrived
we called him Jelly Belly
yelling "cold cock 'em" every
five minutes challenging all
takers in pre-practice kicking.

Saw Jim Lithen's leaping twisting
catches from scrambling Cal Case.
Felt crunching blocks from
Sam Crowe and Butch Eberhardt.
Remember LB Dunn getting
his bell rung prompting
fascinating sideline conversation.

Players cherish their senior year
strapping it on one last time
hoping to win 'em all
be Tomahawk Conf. champs.

Quarterback Jim Crozier went
down opening night testing
out mettle bringing setbacks
rebounding in blizzard mania
at Farwell losing punts in
swirling snow anxiously chasing
Larry Esterline razzing Bob Youngman

wearing green mittens knit
by his grandma in Wyoming.

Vividly remember our big play
Button Hook Right Trailer
brought Steve Baker three TDs
at Beal, Barryton, Coleman.
Best game ever was
Dad's Night vs. Harrison's two-ton
line of beef in snow 10 inches deep.
Six guys scored six bangers
Ron Lloyd nailed five PAT's
seeing dads going crazy
pumping hands slapping backs
my dad drew first blood
off a sweet halfback pass
best one came with Sard Bigford
intercepting a pitchout
taking it the other way
the first time his dad
ever saw him play.

Kept coming back watching
new Eagles seeing Terry Wooten
smack down runners and Tom Chappell
run to All-State honors.

Saw Dave Duddles snare
unreachable passes marveled at
Barry Prelipp's sweep right 97 yards
casting off safeties like flies.

Didn't see much for several
seasons spent coaching but
always reading the Press
catching barbershop replays
finding old teammates had

kids playing now.

Came back in recent years
caught epic battles with Beal,
Frankfort, McBain, All-Saints
enjoying Cutler's smash mouth offense
using Bontekoe sized convoys
leading Ross Richards and Chris McCrimmon
all the way to the Silverdome.

Football's different now
coaches everywhere coordinating
head-phoning clipboarding videotaping
players wearing plastic armor
like space cadets gloves and all.

Football's still big here
new Eagles proudly display
tough playoff-hungry teams
creating community energy
it's the best show in town
may it always be so.

XIII. The Platters

Love my poet cousin
Terry Wooten's line on
his run at Cadillac's Platters ---
"Didn't find my wife there,
but I tried for four years."

Musical magnetism mixed male
and female teen rock 'n rollers
drawing a thousand pulsating bodies

every Saturday night seeking
to test social graces while
dancing hours-weeks-years away
doing the Bristol Stomp, the Soc,
Twist, Mashed Potato, Hully Gully,
Swim, Fly, Hitchhiker,
Monkey, Jerk, Freddy
and the very popular cheek
huggin' belly-rubbin' slow ones.

Dancing held a fascination
learning new moves shown
on Bandstand combining athletic
endeavors with special beats
lent to our generation by
Jerry Lee, Dion, Bobby Vee,
Roy O, Chuck, Elvis, Sam the Sham,
the Beach Boys, Temptations, Smokey,
Del, Ricky, the Shirelles,
and Little Stevie Wonder.

Girls and guys flocked there
spilling from cars in groups
presenting a teen smorgasbord delight
pouring in from Tustin, LeRoy,
Lake City, Manton, Luther,
Marion (never McBain) and
vacationers seemingly from everywhere
mixing and matching eagerly
searching out fun
acceptance and maybe even
a good night kiss.

Music mixes created chances
some scattering when fast
hot jumpin' tunes blared
leaving floor space for

rockin' whole lot a shakin'
arm pumping shoe sliding
hip-swiveling gyrators
like you know who.

Sweet slow ones magically
changed wild leapers to
smooth gliders even coaxing
wall flowers to bloom
holding swaying side to side
couples stuck together tight
girls closing eyes dreaming
how wonderful love could be
guys testing just where
right hands might go.

All the dancing
all the people
tune after tune
week after week
making Saturday nights special
keeping old friendships alive
finding new ones for
just an hour or two
or the rest of your life.

It's troubling today
seeing kids so aimless
stuck on MT video trash
thinking drunken house parties
make fun ways to meet
there's really no place
to go to find other kids
who just want
to have fun.

XIV. Ronzo the Two-Handed Jacker

Nicknames can come strangely
unusual actions - character trait - flawed skills
dubious deeds done - crazy happenings begot
Shorty, Bubbles, Shooter, Leaper,
Lurch, Skunk, Cannibal, Lips,
Birddog, Moonie, the Puker.

Two-handed jacker hooked
onto me one icy slippery
Saturday night stranded behind
The Platters dance hall flat tire
stickin' us to frozen dirt
while saucy Cincinnati snowbunnies
drove off to burger land
pursued by every silver-tongued
birddog from LeRoy to Lake City.

Ronzo wasted no time
mourning bad luck launching
a hubcap-poppin' nut-spinnin' tire iron
slamming jack to frame
catching loud moans from by-standers
"No! the other rear's flat too."

Less experienced hands wouldn't
carry two jacks, two spares, blankets,
blocks, baling wire, flashlights
we been there before.

Now two jacks locked in
blocks chucked in front
handles pumping jacks clicking
alternately raising Ole Green

perilously on ice.

Jacking both sides at once
left-right left-right left-right
chants rose in the frozen night
hands steadying Ole Green
hoping she'd stand still
for this slick double shoeing
retreads pulled off, baldies on
nuts spinning two handed
jacks clicking down right-left
chants echoed loud again.

Ole Green bounced safely down
hard new rears ready to roll
resuming the maiden chase
hoping the race was still on.

Some declared a new record
less than three minutes
double change on ice
in the dark
no-one actually clocked it
but the legend grew
around the Hillcrest Drive-In
amid spirited cries of triumph
- - - Ronzo the Two-Handed Jacker.

PART 2
YOU CALL THIS
ROMANCE?

Introduction

This collection brings back memories of chasing girls. And I do mean chasing. The catching seemed to elude me. I bemoaned that girls just didn't take me seriously. Then one day at lunch in our dorm cafeteria at CMU, a cutie from Pinckney told me the problem. "You are too into bird dogs, shotguns, and fishing poles." Touché.

I. The Girl Next Door

Convenience.
Enemy or ally?
"next door," dummy
"right under yer nose," fool
she was there everyday.

We grew up friends
sometimes fighting bitterly
like the little gang war
my pelting her backside
with used sparkplugs
she sending a rock upside my head.

Meeting to walk to school
together everyday talking
on who's cool or not,
helping me with
clumsy social graces
helping her with
writing and math.

Would we ever be
together like young couples
seeking puppy love companions
or just stroll as pals
seeing a hundred movies
dancing a thousand times
always looking and talking
about someone else.

High School's cruel
slamming great expectations
with cold reality

girls want older men
juniors and seniors swooping
down on our freshman honeys
leaving us standing
gaping and lost.
She was lost that first fall
chased and caught by
Varsity players not
wasting time on J.V.'s
still friends but never
in the same way.

School days passed forging
trails in different directions
she went steady
nailing her security meant
holding a real job
driving a big Chevy
while my days bounced
between ballgames and
younger maidens thinking
I was particularly cool.

Never even went to
see her wedding day
played ball in Mesick
forgetting old visions
that it would be us
walking down the aisle
like we'd walked
a thousand other places
a million years ago.

II. Last Dance

Back in those days kids
played 45s in the high school gym
dancin' during lunch hour
letting Chuck Berry and Buddy Holly
chase winter chills away.

While winter died slowly
defectors slipped outside
rushing spring playing baseball
amid lingering snow drifts
letting the music play on
for girls lingering inside hoping
noon romance would blossom.

He was lured outside
smelling Neatsfoot oil
feeling the sweet sting
of horsehide smacking leather
hearing the crack of
getting solid wood ring
in his ears while his
mind held dreams of
playing on the brilliant
green of Briggs Stadium

She clutched a dream too
looking over her shoulder
hoping he'd come to her
for at least a fleeting moment
a chance to be together
hating that damn baseball.

He knew she waited there

refusing bird-dogging suitors
certain he'd give up that
last turn at bat for her.

He'd time it perfectly
dashing from field to gym
just in the nick of time
wrapping her with sweaty arms
holding her hand with fingers
blackened from rubbing dirt
up and down the bat handle
like boys did back then.

She took him dirt 'n all
a tell-tale smirk sent
directly to her girlfriends
saying 'I told you so'
just as the faculty DJ
announced the last dance.

III. Real Kissin'

Anticipation
may be almost as good
as actually swappin' spit
wondering what she'll
taste like feel like
where it might go
Real Kissin'!

We're not talkin' casual kissin'
Like Aunt Mona's lipstick laden
smooches just cause she's
so darn glad to see ya

or Grandma's birthday pecks
on the cheek nice
for their sentiment but
not for discussion here.

We're talkin' real wet ones
passion included
lips apart slow sinuously
deep drawing your breath
away to images of ecstasy
kisses.

Girls often reflect I'm told
on their first real kiss
having special significance
like some tribal ritual
akin to bagging your first buck.

Do you remember your first
real lip smackin' body clinchin'
pucker sucker passionate kiss
or have memories clouded over
dimming your magical moments?

Mine came one sultry summer
night at the Swimmin' Hole
with a Yooper from Wakefield
we came up for air together
on the sand bar in midstream
lacking experience
in romantic ventures
practically missing our first shot
almost chipping a tooth
finally connecting trying hard
to make it good.

How about you!

Memories still intact?

Author's Note: This original title of this poem was "First Kiss," but Millennium editor Jim Lithen changed it to "Real Kissin'." Can't argue that.

IV. Yooper Girl

Flowing blond curls
draped over a smiling
round face enveloping
laughing blue eyes
that danced along
the soda fountain counter.

My mind quickly honed
sharply on the point.
New Girl in Town!
Trying to be cool
meant ordering something
catchy and impressionable -
lime soda with chocolate ice cream.

Would such boldness
even be noticed
by this Scandinavian goddess
here-to-fore visualized in novels
adored on the Big Screen
in Viking movies where
Nordic raiders captured
voluptuous maidens in loose furs.

Slurping lime and chocolate
hardly held her attention
but the magazine rack

showing Tuesday Weld and Tab Hunter
embracing the cover of *Seventeen*
stopped her long enough
for us to meet.

Summer romances move fast
days and nights run together
fleeing quickly
as the search for love
races the parting time
on a collision course.

We danced at the Park Pavilion
took evening Mill Pond dips
played euchre and canasta
allowing us to hold hands
settling for goodnight kisses
under her Aunt's porch light.

Time outraced our fun
dooming a summer romance
splitting us on two peninsulas
joined by Big Mac but
separating Yooper Girl and the
Troll from under the Bridge.

Summer romances brew
fall storms of letters
swirling down blizzard-like
changing to spring trickles
finally dripping to a stop.

Yooper Girl didn't
return next summer
like promises gone awry
summer romances seem to end
only to be born again

in a different form.

V. Prom Night

The first time I asked her
she stared in disbelief
that I'd dare ask her
made me proud but
her refusal left me empty.

Days later a friend whispered,
"ask her again."
This time, the smiles came
and the clasping of hands.

I'd been to her house -
the house of my best friend
a thousand times before
groping for what to say
made it seem like the first time.

My eyes quickly caught the scene
dad guarding the door
Grams with camera ready
the bright yellow dress
and long, dark hair
but no Gus in sight.

social graces clouded by doubt
I blurted out, "Gus around?"
and spun the banister
racing up the stairs
three at a time like always.

"Flowers for me," Gus smirked?
"No, stupid, for your sister."
"My sister's going out with you?"
Left him rolling on the floor
clutching his stomach.

Slowly returning downstairs
made me painfully aware
that she and Dad and Grandma
still stood uneasily by the door.

I've forgotten the rest
of my first prom night
but my opening line
has lived on for years
through many barbershop tellings
and guffaws from her dad and mine,
"Gus around?"

VI. Forbidden Love

Ann Landers had a booklet
Fifteen Ways to Tell -
True Love or Hormones?
I need one titled
Forbidden Love -
Why You Can't Have It.

Send $1 with self-addressed
stamped envelope to bring
relief to the victim
of a teenage crush.

She came my junior year

not the flashy type
seen on covers of drug store
novels hanging out of sequin
gowns hoping to catch you
looking and reaching for $1.95.

But her allure deftly
captured me pulling
my senses into a whirlpool
spinning my mind
American Literature losing to her charms.

Focusing on Cotton Mather or John Bunyon
while those snappy green eyes lit
painted lips mouthing Pilgrim's Progress
was hardly something manageable.

Two weeks bird-dogging
sharpened the senses to her smell
her innocent giggle
her swaying skirt passing
through narrow aisles returning
themes casually floated
to perfect desktop landings.

First after game dance
acted as a Mecca luring
rock and roll faithfuls
to twist and shout away
school doldrums and another
frustrating loss to Evart.

Spirits lifted quickly upon
discovering her presence
adorning the stereos equipment
sifting through 45's
selecting the next music mix.

Dancing with a chaperone
usually an act of courage
would draw knowing glances
from teammates and girls alike
aware the crush consumed me.

Hand Ballard's "Twist"
launched shoes in tumbling flight
piling into a corner
away from hips spinning
above white socks
glowing in dim gym light.

Her smooth, graceful pivots
designed not to draw
comment or stare

contrasted ours trying to wear
pants out from the inside.

Then slow, sweet strains
from Skeeter Davis floated floorward
drawing couples magnetically
together mouthing words
in a mock sing along to
"The End of the World."

We fell into an easy
side to side sway, wondering
how close to dance
with an English teacher?
did she have to be MY teacher?

She talked continuously
ruining the mood
slow dancing creates
killing any chance to pretend

there's romantic attraction.

Much that came flowing out
was better not known -
boyfriend near Chicago -
likes visiting on weekends -
may get engaged over X-mas -
. . .on and on and on.

Her excitement went unshared
reality slammed Skeeter's
final words in my face
ending more than a song
"Don't say 'No,

It's the end of the world.'"
"It ended when I lost your love."

Author's Note: This one brought some fun. It was first published in the Marion Millenium by editor Jim "Gus" Lithen, who challenged readers to come up with the name of this teacher from the '60's. Many locals and even guys as far away as Florida tried. The following month's issue brought the answer: Helmboldt had made it all up.

VII. Cover Girls

Enjoyed hanging out at
Van de Warker's Drug Store where
magazine covers stared enticingly
saying *Hi There! Buy me!*
Freely entertaining cover watching
nonbuyers like me.

Covers on girl mags like

Seventeen, Redbook, Glamour,
drew guys in clusters
ogling freely but not
caught dead buying those
sticking to real men stuff
Outdoor Life, The Sporting News, Motor Trend.

Lookers - readers - buyers
didn't seem to match
except for exotic *Playboy*
hidden in a special drawer
saved for certain young men.

Didn't see much skin
on '50's covers 'cept
July 'n August beach shots
leaving to the imagination
what now bares out
as regular competition.

Seductive personal features
lured me to the rack
Sandra Dee's pouty lips
Liz Taylor's snapping eyes
Rita Hayworth's radiant locks
Bridgette Bardot' obvious intelligence
Sofia Loren's catlike mystery
- - - and then there
was Marilyn Monroe!

Guys verbally trashed her
like a common town slut
knowing they'd crawl the Sahara
to look up her skirt
posting that full-bodied siren
on walls, in trucks, at work.

Cover girls came and went
some like Liz an' Rita
lasted decades while others
flashed brilliantly only to
burn out before becoming
Tuesday Weld or Audrey Hepburn.

Those glossy paper love
affairs were great fun
sparking lively conversations
giving males everywhere something
for debate allowing daydreams
to carry us away
with our own cover girl.

My favorite found me and
Natalie Wood meeting in Cadillac
she stopping for a burger
me sweeping us away
escaping Hollywood madness
finding small town bliss
in a new trailer on M-66.

VIII. Miss Manton

Lake City 4th of July parade
pulled folks in from miles
like flies to manure, Gramps said.

The part I liked best
featured local queens perched
on Chamber of Commerce floats.

The 1963 highlight caught
bright sun rays dancing on raven hair
sweet-looking lips, the laughing eyes
belonging to Miss Manton.

My vision, my consciousness
captured by her chârm
Pied Piper stuff
pulling me down the sidewalk
hooked to the parade.

Parades disbanded in the school lot
where I happened to turn up
hoping to question those eyes.
Was the float smile real?
Would those lips talk to me?

Smiling small talk led to
examining and probing questions
like a dreaded pop quiz
making you think on your feet.

Able to dance
later at the Pavilion
rockin' and rollin' and Jerry Lee
moved us in a twist and shout mode
hoping the Righteous Bros.
would be along soon.

Watching fireworks with caramel corn
Coca-Cola and cotton candy
spawned a brief summer romance
cooled by fall college classes.

My still warm coals
hoped to rekindle flames
returning the heat of summer.

to make memories live again.

Homecoming brought unwanted chills
the cold winds of fall and the news
she was engaged--
should I laugh or cry?
. . .to the guy pumping gas
at the Speedway truck stop.

IX. Having to Choose

Bouncing down dusty
truck rattling dirt roads
leaving brown clouds drifting
across scruffy Jack Pine plains
hard to listen, think and steer.

Willie Nelson's nasal tones
cut the dust simplifying
complicated triangular puzzles.
"Why do I have to choose?"
"Make everybody lose."
"It's giving me the blues."
"Well, this time, I refuse!"

The young one had laughing eyes
thin, lithe body
bouncing around her yard
springing hands to feet
mouthing cheers to a pretend game.

The newcomer had grit
blue collar factory girl
strong frame built

stacking feed sacks and hay bales
tantalizing under tight jeans.

One easy to date
waiting eagerly for calls
watching for the honking
waving truck to fly past
knowing Saturday night was hers.

The other one made fun
gathering after-work friends
cruising Cadillac burger joints
leading chasing guys to think
they might catch her.

What forces draw us
away from sweet, loyal dates
waiting conveniently homebound
to follow seductively scented trails
often crossed by birddogging pursuers?

How to play a double header
both games at once
caused a summer juggling act
testing creative skills
holding one caged dove
while trapping the wild she-hawk
simultaneously.

Holding on while chasing
sapped strength drawing energy
taxing friendships driving wedges
between supporters of green eyes
or factory girl.

"Burning the rope at both ends,"
"End up with neither."

warned predictors supposedly
experienced in such matters.

But how to choose?
Willie's words spun often—
like the turntable—
carrying doubts but reminding
virtues belonged to both.

The dreaded triangle scene
fell into place one hot
sweaty summer Saturday night
where young dancers met
to inspect and expect
something good.

Fast songs allowed maneuvering
magically using crowd cover
slipping from one to the other
promising each the next
slow dance.

"California Dreaming" caught me
between both beauties converging
eying each other spewing
dagger-like curses sticking me
with valuable tips on
places to go and how to get there.

The Mamas and Papas crooned
sweetly about California -
hardly far enough for
safety from flying pieces
of a fragmented triangle.

Oh, for a quiet ride
down some lonely country road

filtering Willie's words
floating through dusty clouds
wondering will I even
have the chance to choose?

X. Struck Out

Her eyes drifted across time
beyond ball field antics
back to last summer's bliss
her Bobby-Love solidly wrapped
around her ring finger
unbothered by baseball madness
infecting the chattering man - boys
she now listlessly watched.

Betsy cast smiling half-sneers
toward her first baseman brother
glad he could find such
simple pleasure taking infield
sweeping his flopping webbed mitt
snapping errant throws gracefully
dancing twisted pirouettes
having the time of his life
mad he didn't share
her humiliating hurt.

Bobby-Love pledged his vows
marrying a Jenny-come-lately
leaving her stranded watching
foolish flannel-clad players
fighting tears meant to
cleanse bitter rejection.

Her sad eyes pretended
to watch ballplayers but
longed for another time
another place another mile
down the road where Bobby 'n Linda
danced as one at the VFW hall.

Betsy sat trying to
hold a breaking heart together
leaving a shortstop and second baseman
shooting barbs at one another
each laying claim she
had come to watch him.

During an eighth-inning rally
bringing the hometown nine
back from near defeat
horns honked down M-66
announcing Bobby 'n Linda's departure
to honeymoon bliss leaving
Betsy's trembling hands to
applaud her brother's victory
knowing love had struck her
out.

XI. Double-edged Sword

Damn that sword
that double-edged sword
one blade constantly cutting
little pieces off my heart
when I can't be near you.

Then the other blade

slices more pieces
when you are because
I can't touch you
can't kiss kiss kiss
all over your body
can't love you.

Damn that sword
that double-edged sword
and damn me for failing
to find a way to
stop the nagging pain
my heart carries every day.

Don't know how many
pieces are left to cut.

*Author's Note: The idea for this one came from a real student-teacher crush a friend
experienced at CMU. It didn't work out and he cried in his beer at the Horseshoe
Bar in Marion.*

XII. College Babes

Heading for college
stirs many emotions
tugging conflicting strings
tightening your heart.

Trading nests holding
friendly familiar faces
for unknown encounters
searching new faces in strange places.

Local sweethearts left
standing porchside wondering
what direction love will take
was a tug-of-war
pulling me back.

Campus impressions loomed
monster-like ready to swallow
hicktown wonderboys in awe
. . .Big Dorms, Big Cafeterias, Big Lecture Halls,
Big Doubts.

Relief came at mealtime
mixing our dorm
with sisters next door
thrusting us together
for close examination.

Eyes longingly searched
this co-ed smorgasbord
sizing, grading, checking out
possible mutually attractive subjects

to meet, to know, to like,
or just talk about.

Several eye-catchers passed daily
keeping spirits high
bringing hope and realization--
This place would be
All Right!

One stole the show
separating herself easily
drawing magnetic stares
producing boasts, promises, predictions.

This bashful brunette beauty
shoved thoughts of hometown honeys
to warm on the back burner
wondering if love would last.

How to meet one desired
by a hundred hungry sharks
swirling around their prey
presented a difficult dilemma.

'Better lucky than good'
worked for me this time
seems her roomie and mine
shared biology class making
a study date foursome foray.

Talking for hours while
sharing many meals
coaxed shared tidbits
learning we liked walks,

dancing, Johnny Rivers, the Tigers
and someone back home.
Professing loyalty homeward
contradicted growing fondness
providing a safety net
preventing a fall for freshmen
unsure where a new
love might lead.

Sharing Cokes over miles
strolling campus neighborhoods
talking of future dreams
among falling leaves pulled
us together hand in hand.

Winter wants couples together

fighting cold winds
forgetting hometown heartthrobs
expecting our loyalty
to keep the fire burning.

Spring blooms brash feelings
mixing love, deadlines, exams
then sends us home, but
to or from our love?

Parting found us fearing
losing our carefully cultivated
newly budding romance
risking all on an unknown course
divided by summer
challenged by love left home.

She never returned
staying home working
building her own nest
leaving me in new cafeteria lines
to study and with more experienced eyes -
eyes schooled in the way
of College Babes.

XIII. Keeper

She swept into our halls
long silky hair swaying
perky bouncing steps
tantalizing short skirts.

Football pulled us
along a common thread

backfield coach and cheer advisor
together after the game
changed my life abruptly
leaving roaming bachelor habits
channeling loose, drifting ways
to pursue higher class game.

No rules govern when
lives change beginning
serious mating rituals
hoping one finds another
holding mutual desires
wanting their life to
take the same turn.

Saw a Hollywood type vision
fate as a big white horse
carrying us away together
riding double into the sunset
happily ever after.

My best friend saw it
in her understanding eyes
watching me leap up
replaying Jesse Lake's TD run
in a CMU watering hole
spilling two gin 'n tonics
on her new suede jacket
producing nary a howl
confiding "she is really
in love with you!"

Cupid finally shot straight
stopping cold aimless nights
sticking a love-tipped
arrow thru two hearts.

Ron Helmboldt

Our teacher/coaching year
passed quickly enough
having planning hour together
helped ease constant yearnings
to see her every day.

So much together by spring
planning June wedding bells
celebrating joining different people
different families different churches
even different ministers blending
all ingredients into one.

Nearly lost in confusion
I found a real keeper
nest-building lover
mother of my children
conscience for my soul.

P.S. And now, after 44 years, a four-time grandmother!

PART 3
THE GREAT OUTDOORS

Introduction

Doing things in the outdoors, whether it was just roaming around playing or seriously hunting elk, has always been a part of me. Caught my first brookie at four, got my first hunting dog at five, first shotgun at nine, etc.

Where I grew up, open fields and woods were out the back door. I indulged freely and frequently. I hunted and fished with my grandparents, dad, uncles, cousins, friends, and neighbors. When we weren't out there in nature, we had hundreds of stories about such in my Grandpa Fred's and father Mel's Barbershop. This was our life.

I'm fortunate to be able to hunt deer and fish lakes, streams, piers, and ice in my seventies. This collection reflects my love of the outdoors. It's just better outside.

I. Everett's Story

Stung twice that spring
by sharp Eagle Claw hooks
the burly brown grew wary
selectively feeding during dark
quiet times using stealth
ambushing Mayflies, minnows, crayfish
like a thief in the night.

Several guys knew this trout
knew his lair his muscle
had felt his power
knew the challenge of
coaxing a strike and
luring him from his
root-infested cavern hideout
beyond their grasp.

The barber came here often
waiting to see the big guy
drop his guard carelessly
when caddis offered floating
feeding frenzies fish fell
for fortuitously.

Sometimes he just sat
smoking a cigarette resting
tired legs massaged
by cool current carrying
aches from his feet
watching the skyline where
dancing fish flies mated
over the water.

This night it happened early
flies were quickly dropping
hungry mouths rose swirling
to steal tasty morsels
seemingly before they even
hit the water.

The barber worked cautiously
slowing inching upstream careful
not to send a wake
alarming the big brown
putting him down to hide.

The big boy came out too
not splashing and thrashing
like noisy showy youngsters
but gently easing up
making subtle slurping sounds
the barber knew well.

The fly line rode along
flowing loops to and fro
extending itself to reach
above the bend where
he had to cast to
fool the big one.

It all came together
in a surprising way
as the fly sailed through
the evening sky a leaf
fluttered down to the river
an instant before the
fly landed.

Amazing coincidence had the
fly landing on the leaf

in a casting phenomenon.

Knowing the trout couldn't
see his fly he prepared
to lift his fly away.

Lady luck prevailed when
river current spun the leaf
causing the fly to slide
discretely into the big guy's
feeding lane fooling him.

Barber and trout hooked
into each other pulling
toward opposite poles each
determined to win brownie
driving toward deep cover
the barber backing away
throbbing rod held high.

Brownie tired and turned
facing the relentless pressure
swimming into waiting net
to be lifted skyward
by a superior force.

The barber waded back
to his seat on the bank
his heart raced excitedly
the trout swam slowly
along in the net.

Flashlight beams showed healed
scars on both lips
revealing past battles won
lips now gasping for life
seemed to be mouthing words

"It was that damned leaf.
Completely faked me out."

The barber spoke
"Okay, Big Guy. Guess
it wasn't a fair fight,"
then slipped brownie
back into the river.

Author's Note: This poem is based on a story retold by a chuckling Everett Verrett as he remembered hearing it one day while waiting for a hair cut. The stranger in the chair was mesmerized. Everett often wondered if Mel really caught that big brown, but he did reel in that city boy.

II. Buck and Shot

Whoever said "happiness is
a warm puppy" understood
simple basic pleasure gained
from round warm little bellies
floppy ears slurping tongues
waggling tails and busy feet
carrying noses constantly sweeping
grounds for new scent.

When Grandpa's hound Peg
spilled nine squirming beagles
onto a straw pile little
rat-like shut-eyed creatures
drew family hunters honed
sharp in pickin' the litter.

Not knowing how pickin's
decided who would get

which pup didn't phase me
mine just seemed to
stick to my hand
like magic.

Each probe into a dark coop
amongst wriggling fur balls
pulled the same pup out
time after time.

Pick 'o the litter theories
flew fast some freely given
others closely guarded
lookin' in the mouth
checkin' the feet, hips
watchin' every move
made going for food
sniffing the grass, etc.

I just kept grabbing
one smallish imp
no tell-tale white markings
nor attractive traits
mine by unpopular demand
what did I know
at only five years old?

Dad picked one too
had all the right stuff
guaranteed huntin' fool
Shot ran rabbits at
three months old while
Buck had a puzzled look
on that perfectly marked
face for two years.
We grew into hunting naturally
those dogs teaching me

romping thru weed fields
brushy swales, potholes, pines
taking me across sections
getting me lost but always
taking me home.

Those two became the best
rabbit runnin' beagles
known far and wide thru
barbershop storytelling witnessed
by many shotgunners blessed
to hark their soprano/bass mixture
sweet wood music ringing
out the joy of the chase.

This partnership lasted
fifteen great years much
to the chagrin of hundreds
of cottontails but providing
outdoor pleasure few
men/boys will ever know.
It has not happened

like that again but I
never expected it would.

III. Ghost Crick

Heard the scary stories
Shoot the Cat Osborn's ghost
lurked as an eery light
bouncing along the track
hovering over the crick
guarding his natural treasures

partridge, rabbits, deer, brook trout.

Catching ghostly brookies meant
applying the AFTER rule - - -
after a good rain
after dark
after season for some scoundrels.

Best fished alone meant
ditching Blackie the Schwinn
secretly behind roadside brush
quick stepping RR ties
two at a time heading
up the tracks to probe
ghostly quiet, dark gurgling water.

Carefully ducking and sliding
thru bankside tangles to
entice wary brookies floating
worms gently into cover holes
treading lightly testing patience
never disturbing natural presence
plucking radiant trout out
to wiggle in bankside grass.

My fifthteenth summer brought
enough daring courage to
fish Ghost Crick alone in darkness
finding bigger trout but
always feeling watched sending
cold shivers down my neck
childlike boogyman fears wondering
would the ghostly lantern
shine on me tonight?

Whistling RR songs helped
"Casey Jones" worked quite well

repelling the ghost who favored
silence over lout off-key renditions
proving noise to be good
ghost repellent but attractive
tonic to bloodthirsty skeeters.

Growing older changes how
evenings are spent making
forays to Ghost Crick seemed
foolishly anti-social void of
girls, cheeseburgers, or rock-n-roll
rendering the place considerably
less cool.

Reflecting back in time
now leaves me thinking
Ghost Crick actually oozed coolness
leaving yearnings rarely satisfied
by today's recreational endeavors
causing me to wonder
is ole Osborn's ghost
still haunting the creek?
does anyone fish there?
could you just play a
Johnny Cash cassette blasting
"Orange Blossom Special"
instead of whistling or singing?

IV. Fish Date

Ever go fishing with a girl?
There's mixed emotions
right from the start.

You can like both
equally hard but
not at the same time
do we talk date or bait?
do we fish to impress
or just hope to caress?

Such a dilemma happened
one steamy July night
amid hatching bugs
swirling bats and Jeanne
with the light brown hair.

Better judgment said
to separate the pole
from the stroll
but mayfly hatches
come and go
hot or cold
like Jeanne was wont to do.

Would fishing be bonding glue
holding us together
pulling us toward common love?
Love for pursuit of game?

"Not hardly," buzzed
ten thousand mosquitoes
"Not even close," whistled

a darting bat flitting
ever so close to her hairdo
"Forget it completely,"
whispered the mouse
while he scampered
over Jeanne's pantleg.
Should I have to say
we left posthaste
no brookies in the bag
no illusions of great
angling experiences
to be retold in tales
of stream-side love.

Our dates slowed
like beaver dam current
trapped until stagnant
Jeanne caught the flow
of a different stream
carrying an engagement ring.

I fished on
catching many brookies while
sharing the love of environs
common to me and
my speckled friends.

V. Just Beautiful

Initial impressions said
love at first sight
big round brown eyes
followed you everywhere
capturing your heart.

Perfect chest
strong enough and firm
coming at you
showing the right ripples.

Easy graceful stride
watchable from any angle
giving perfect companionship
on walking trails
meant for friends.

Rear view, too
produced complementary smiles
admiring guys watching
muscular hips swaying
side to side.

Beautiful
Just beautiful
Best lookin' coon dog in six counties.

VI. Mind Surfing

Deer stands promote mind surfing
sitting quietly hardly moving
eyes searching nook and cranny
hours spent alone causes
minds to drifts like clouds
flit like chickadees changing
subjects randomly seemingly without
hope for focus or plan.

Such a mind surfing session
flowed through my hunter orange hat

while perched high on canyon wall
several miles outside Craig, Colorado
gorgeous crisp breezy day
deer still bedded in oakbrush
mind free to float to linger
when a subject seemed worthy.

First, it was food when my
stomach growled its empty protest
thoughts of ordering something juicy
at Craig's Bad to the Bone Grill
swearing I could smell brisket
now prime rib then hot coffee
wow get off food I
told my brain when ice
cold wind swirled around
blowing food away like
fleeting snowflakes bringing
visions of warmer climes.

Golden sands of Ocean City beaches
drifted in bringing bikinis
bouncing down boardwalks thinking
that's more like it!
Purple Moose Saloon with Joe
Cocker and Three Dog Night blaring
jukebox beats waitresses
wearing really thin tops
encouraging another round but
another cold blast and poof ...

Beaches gone replaced by Jim
Reeves singing "The Blizzard"
how did that happen?
his song clearly playing like
he's on the rock beside me
there were " hot biscuits

in the pan" at Mary Ann's
but he "just couldn't leave
old Dan" so there I saw
him "hands frozen to
the reins," "just 100 yards
from Mary Ann's" holy crap
flush that mind bender out.

Thoughts continued to change
visions came and went like
birds looking for a better bush
then suddenly there he was
beautiful muley buck walking
through open sage searching
ahead for trouble not seeing
the hunter above him now
zeroed in on business at hand.

VII. Deer Camp Lingo

Richly tainted vocabulary contained
lessons to be learned
from deer camp lingo
wisdom passed thru generations
stories retold on how
to bag your buck.

My experience started early
eldest grandson privileges
visiting Uncle Tone's cabin
opened eyes and ears
to life deer camp style
swearing belching farting dealing
cards and whiskey while

expounding hunting tidbits.

"Third base the (insert expletive)"
boldly growled a Durand cousin
cleverly combining baseball expression
with deer hunting and penchant
for nailing said buck
before he got to
another waiting hunter
hence you third based him
before he could score.

"Shit in my crosshall"
reflected remorse over
double-crossing dirty pool
(like getting third based)
having your runway
rudely intruded upon by
some stumble-bum late crasher
lousing up well-scouted plans
didn't reflect actual
defecation on said location
but might as well have.

"Don't marry the cook"
applied to those choosing
cooking culinary camp delights
over guarding swamp crossings
bringing warnings that bucks
weren't bagged by spatula
wooden spoons or Bisquick.

"Went to shit and
the hogs ate him"
suited any occasion where
time dallied away idly
lost precious moments at stand

applying literally to Uncle Dude
known for spending lingering
minutes stuck in the outhouse
delaying impatient partners
thinking he had to be
permanently wedged in a hole.

"Piss on the fire
'n call the dogs"
stirring call to action
moved people convincingly
into the task at hand
usually a big drive
organized by battle strategists
capable of moving small armies
thru classic buck hideouts
the Armour Land, Arnold's Swails, Turl Swamp,
Forbe's Corner, Sanford's Pines, or
the Mott Foundation property.

Deer camp instilled
good habits for life--
cooking and dishes
tending the fire
when to raise or fold
don't trump your partner's ace
sharpening knives cutting meat
smoking jerky...
...but the best lessons learned
centered around deer camp lingo.

VIII. Love Those Brookies

Remember your first trout?
Mine came accidentally
a four-year-old left
standing at a bridge
others finding good holes
along Ryan's crick
getting yelled at
"quit kicking stones
in the crick" as my
little 8-inch brookie
frantically splashed below.

Brook trout hooked me good
we became very tight
taking me enchanted places
Middle Branch, Clam, Butterfield
hidden creeks closely guarded
Caesar's, Ghost, Fran's, Green.

Little ones dart to bait
flashing speed-agility-hunger-fear
offering light resistance heroically
showing off remarkable beauty
color shades changing
crick to crick
even hole to hole.

Grew up thinking every guy
could read moving water
dunk worms in the dark
spit skeeters an' bite sinkers
slingshot a squirrel tail fly
sidearm under tag alders.

Age hampers brookie reunions
harder to walk that mile
ladened in waders' n gear
harder to avoid warning signs:
"Keep Out," "Posted,"
"Trespassers Will Be Violated."

Me 'n brookies still meet
 mostly in my mind
cherishing sweet memories
good times spent sharing
those magnetic hallowed environs
carefully extracting speckled gold
wishing we could be
that close again.

IX. Twin Eights

Through thick willow clumps
high yellow swamp grass
twins silently slipped ghost-like
morning fog screening their bodies
masking true identity of those
delicate eight point antlers.

In a breath quick instant
after the leader had
faded safely from sight
the trailer fatefully showed
his antlered headgear.

Precious seconds spent lingering
cost the young buck his life
snuffed out too quick with

one white-hot flash of lead.

Twins now halved
left one bewildered following
patterned routes like clockwork
down the same trail at sunset
past the same hunter ready.

Dropping just five yards away
from his brother's deathbed
meant the twin eights changed
forms no longer alive but
serving to feed the hunter
by the table and soul alike.

X. Two Hawks

Long shrill shrieks sent chills
down small furry necks
making the crisp sunrise
seem even colder causing
nervous eyes to search the sky
sending feet scurrying home.

Somewhere up there high
search hunting over grasses
flashing tandem jet-like shadows
cruised two hawks
screaming death warnings to
rabbits mice gophers squirrels.

Flying as though connected
on a long elastic cord
drifting far apart

only to be pulled back
nearly touching wingtips
dipping rising soaring diving
together for life and death
two hawks.

XI. Take Me I'm Yours (Ode to the Morel Mushroom)

Can't you see me?
I'm right here
Hey! Are you blind?
You think I'm
some kind of wallflower?
I'm only inches from
your big hard boot
you clumsy ox
would you rather
crush me underfoot
than savor my delights
mixed in your omelette
sizzling with your steak
prompting the oohs and aahs
that follow me everywhere.

I said, Hey!
I'm right here
next to the rotting
maple log dressed in
my brown crinkled cape
looking fresh as new grass
can't you see me?
You just gonna walk
right on by gaping
at flashy trilliums

radiant white while
I'm plain Jane
brown fungus but Hey!
I could be yours
for a quick look
a slight pause
ripe for picking
but you keep walking
distracted by the scent
the beauty of prettier ones.

Make sure you understand
you're the big loser buddy.

XII. Wapiti

North American Elk
Cervus elaphus
sought for millennia
hunted for substance and thrill
not for fame or ego
but a true trophy
gained thru honest ethics
earned from mutual respect
bringing honor to Wapiti.

Ogalala Holyman Black Hawk
taught Wapiti to be sacred
holding mysteries of life
possessing magical powers
like seeds planted in
dark soil reaching lightward
like seeds planted in
wombs to grow life

creates some share of eternity
like the spirit
of Wapiti.

XIII. The Intricate Mistress

Shameless in her insatiable desire
she constantly beckons to me
demanding her share of attention
calling out from highlands
asking to roll thru hills
ride across oak ridges
even inviting the dog
can you imagine that?

She waves from trees
offering seductive panoramic views
prickling subtle senses keen
to sneaky antlered whitetail.

She likes it wet, too
sloshing in tributaries carrying
salmon to their rites of fertility
spawning amid radiant colors
reflecting her beauty off
the glassy shimmering surface
or hiding with you in cattails
promising a crack at mallards
whistling by swaying treetops.

She can be moody
dressed radiantly in sunlit brightness
then throwing a tantrum
a dark, surly cold-shoulder

chasing all the faint hearted.

She is complicated and relentless
She is the mistress of intrigue
She is October.

XIV. Buzzard Breath

We met along the line fence
he perched on a corner post
me cutting up the draw
to catch the trail leading
me to the way home.

He was so ugly
it shook my innards
to see his ghostly
red-lined haunting face
staring rather lifeless
not showing panic or
giving signs of flight.

My walk slowed deliberately
the encounter being both
spooky and fascinating in the
startling closeness neither
me nor the buzzard
had ever experienced before.

His rancid stink
stopped me cold leaving
us in a quandary
him not feeling well
after consuming tainted sheep

me growing ill just
from his very presence
causing us to wonder
who was going to
puke first?

PART 4
COLLECTIONS FROM LATER IN LIFE

Introduction

Ideas for these selections came from all over the place, starting with a clarification. "Not a Real Poet" helps describe my writing, as I'm just a storyteller where real poets write profound, complicated stuff. Several of these subjects include stories I heard as a kid. Some came as ideas while traveling. Some just came out of life, like poems for my granddaughters' picture books their dad makes each year.

I. Not a Real Poet

Poets face creative dilemmas
plagued to play word games
causing mere walks on the beach
or strolls in the woods
or star gazing on the pier
to become tangled mental images
words ricocheting bullet-like
trying to hit floating pieces
of philosophical puzzles hiding
life's true meaning behind
waves, trees, stars, drifting sand
leaving the poet cursed
wrestling with universal mysteries.

Could I enter this world—
creating thought-provoking mind-bending
spellbound images magically
transforming everyday Hallmark scenes
sending readers soaring into
soul-searching adventures thinking
they had been moonstruck
by a literary genius?

Apparently not.
My work instead seems
tracked to storytelling reminisces
serving readers nostalgic doses
kindling old memory sparks
meaning more to me
than anyone else.

Realizing Walt Whitman's not
about to jump outta my skin

brings more relief than disappointment
allowing simple moments to remain
pleasurable chances to reflect
rather than publisher pressured
gut-wrenching challenges demanding
profound production suitable for
print and profit.

Such pressure whether self-imposed
or corporate in origin
burdens those gifted literary marvels
depriving them pleasures easily
enjoyed by the simple minded
but possibly elevating them
to another level of being
beyond our ability to comprehend.

II. Escaping

Laid on my back sunning
along the Middle Branch River
playing the cloud game
creating life from drifting
white masses flowing overhead
South America came slightly tilted
followed by toads and pigs
then a charging buffalo
chased the cloud game
bringing Wild West visions
scouting for Gen. Custer
sneaking along the Little Big Horn
hiding below undercut banks
breathing thru hollow reeds
slipping away amid chaos

the only survivor
fooling history.

III. Imagine That

Couldn't believe it myself but
there sat James Dean smirking
right across my kitchen table
one leg cocked over his knee
squinting through curling cigarette smoke
sipping Old Crow and munching
Saltine crackers smeared with
butter and strawberry jam.

There was so much I wanted
to say to ask to learn
why was he sitting at my table?
Does he ever see Bogie?
Elvis? Louis Armstrong?
And Marilyn! I was dying
to ask about Marilyn mostly
Are those big luscious things
as sweet as they look?
-- her lips, I mean.

But I just couldn't get
anything to come out
the fear of breaking the aura
too strong to deny
too strong to waste
on the chance he'd become
annoyed with my silliness
that we couldn't be pals
'cause I was just another

pesky awestruck fan.

Questions no longer mattered
maybe my concentration slipped
too much on Marilyn but
he took one more sip
and simply vanished.

Imagine that.

IV. Venus and Mars

She glided across the room
shining eyes winking radiantly
gracefully passing stationary bodies
casting a glow on
those in her path.

He watched at a distance
hoping to work closer
to catch some shine too
knowing he would be
hard-pressed to capture her
evasive orbit this night.

She maneuvered through cluttered sky
leaving lesser bodies trailing
eluding him slyly as by
some heavenly elliptical design
allowed close passage yet
kept them apart.

He tried closing the gap
before the night escaped

knowing he couldn't really
make their bodies match
the way he dreamed futilely
night after night.

Suddenly the distance closed
he brushed her backside
sliding by her tail
feeling electric charges that
he hoped would stay
longer than the last time.

She felt it too
felt the blushing heat
felt her chest tighten
wanted to slow down
to make it last longer
than just a quick hot jolt.

But all too rapidly
some gravitational enemy
pulled them apart leaving
their lights still shining
but without the same glow.

Dedicated to daughter-in-law Carrie, a NASA astronomer working on a Mars project, and son Joe, who, as an astronomer at the Naval Research Laboratory, is so far out there I can't explain it.

V. Imaginary Valentine

He stared ahead mesmerized
snow swirled through headlight beams
growing thicker reaching farther into
dark curves and over rolling ridges.

He occasionally reached across
the empty passenger seat sliding
his palm where her thigh
would stretch responding pleasingly
to his warm hand, or
so he imagined.

He fought being alone
not on February 14 not
Valentine's Day when lovers
everywhere ride the road
to romance with flowers
and gifts of affection.

He kept reaching through the darkness
reaching through emptiness that
threatened the spirit of tonight
defying solitude as an enemy
remaining dignified in dejection.

He found Don's Road House cafe
open but deserted by patrons
no longer munching Quirky Turkey
or sipping double caramel mocha·
only the owners remained
readying their own celebration
table set with white candles
red ribbon and Cracklin' Rose.

He left feeling the intruder
interrupting a real Valentine evening
retreating to his lonely abode
hoping cable TV could
salvage some relief filling
the void of impending singleness.

He found TNT's Saturday Night Classics
showing "Dirty Dancing" spotlighting
dreamy music driving pulsating bodies
kissing bumping sliding together
leading his emotions to run
amorously pulling him and his
Imaginary Valentine to the floor
where he felt quite silly
and very much alone.

VI. If I Had a Nickel . . .

Tripping back home along
Ann Arbor RR tracks
had me thinking
"if I had a nickel for
every tie I crossed- - -"
made me sound just
like Grandpa Helmboldt.

He'd spew forth with
"If I had a nickel
for every- - -
- - -brookie I caught in Butterfield Creek
- - -weed I pulled outta them taters
- - -skeeter swatted off my neck

- - -rabbit skinned in the back shed
- - -trip to the outhouse in the dark
- - -time I smoked my last cigarette, etc.
I'd be a rich man!"

That would jump start Grandma
"If I had a nickel
for every- - -
- - -cookie you kids stuffed down
- - -pea shucked-cherry pitted-apple cored, etc.
- - -jar of beans-corn-tomatoes I canned
- - -time I told you kids to wipe yer feet,
I'd be a rich woman!"

By the next generation
stakes were up to a quarter
my dad proclaiming
"If I had a quarter
for every- - -
- - -trout I hauled outta Crocker Hole
- - -peck of taters I put in Bontekoe's storehouse
- - -pat I shot behind Ole Beau
- - -homer I put out at Rose Lake, Frankfort, etc.
- - -time I had to tell you kids to mow, feed the dogs, do the dishes, etc.
I'd never have to work again!"

Such trivial amounts
date these Depression Era
nickel and dimers
now that I've taken over
quoted values have risen
"If I had a buck
for every- - -"

Which proves two points - -
no-one is actually giving
us any of that money;

the older we get
the more we sound like- - -

VII. A Country Music Song

Gonna write a country music
song one of these days
about love gone bad
gonna use some of those
clever lines cycling my mind
stuck in a holding pattern.

Like when me 'n Grampa
were runnin' an hour
late fishin' Butterfield Crick
I'd ask "Grampa, what
do ya think we'll have
for supper when we git home?"

He'd crack a slight smile
old fedora tipped back
way late but toting
a bulging bag of brookies
secured on the floorboard
"'Spect we'll git some of
that hot tongue and
cold shoulder your Gramma serves."
The start of a good
song right there!

Or if we entered a room
finding it unexpectedly cold
my dad would refer to his
childhood bedroom upstairs at

Park Lake where he and his
brother strung rabbits and partridge
by the feet during winter and
he'd say "It's cold enough
in here to hang meat!"

While not too romantic those
lines could fit together
instead of floating aimlessly
hook them to a proper melody
Presto! A future hit
could be born.

When the old Monday Night Football
crew was around and the game
would bog down late and
Dandy Don would break out
with a couple lines of
"If you want to keep
your six pack cold, put it
next to my wife's heart."
means there's probably a hit
going to waste all over
America on any given night.

Yeah, someday those great
lines will flow together
into surefire country hitsville,
making me famous.

VIII. Gone Country

Some dig the New Country sound
others still covet real twang
widening the scope of C & W music
stealing listeners previously stuck on
rock 'n roll, jazz, blues or
floating listlessly on elevator music.

New stars turned the trick
Hank Jr. stole waning rockers
Alan Jackson captured young hearts
Garth thundered to top charts
Reba transcended the entire industry.

Country concerts blossomed hats
fancy boots, western shirts, swaying skirts
sharing space with t-shirted screaming
teens wanting Aaron, Tracy, Travis, Mark
like their mothers once sighed
for Elvis, the Beatles, and the Rolling Stones.

Country's become timely and timeless
one can drift back to founders
Bill Monroe, Roy Acuff, Jimmy Rogers
relive the '50's with Hank Williams,
Hank Snow, Faron Young, Sonny James
enjoy the golden-voiced '60's with
Jim Reeves, Patsy C., Eddy A., Marty R.
Croonin' on barroom jukeboxes
then fast forward to rockin' hot
new polished acts - colored lights,
smoke, electric everything boomin'.

It's all been a revelation

for us old rockers disgusted
by post-1960s crap posing
as music leaving us empty
forcing us to cling to "dead music"
as critics caustically call Oldies.

Country swept in lifting spirits
picking up tired ears
Waylan and Willie, Conway and George Jones
made music alive again
instilling a sense of history
supporting an American tradition
bridging social classes allowing
urban cowboys to grasp
valuable lessons on life
from backwoods country lore.

It's a fresh love affair
mixing old and new passions
hillbilly hayseed twang matched to
sophisticated professional studio productions
picking fat wallets for new CD's
bringing adoring fans to
worship at the Nashville Shrine.

Dedicated to the Cadillac Country Kids, Carol and Jerry Landers, who went country
when this was written in the 90's.

IX. Coal Run

Cold winter winds always
called for more fuel constantly
eating up precious coal reserves
devouring wood piles weekly
leaving cash short Depression
families scavenging anything combustible.

Park Lake hustlers Eddie, Charlie, 'n Mel
hitched a ride or walked
down to Marion wandering streets
waiting out the Ann Arbor train
coming north hoping it'd stop
side-tracked at the feed mill.

Hopping moving freight cars
very tricky at the least
required strength 'n timing
jumping off the ground
before you grabbed railcar
handles prevented your dangling
legs from swinging into
the next car behind.

Once aboard the lads
hid between or inside open
cars trying not to freeze
riding five miles waiting
the long sweeping curve
before Park Lake Depot.

With curve in sight they
sprang into action climbing
onto a coal car rolling

big chunks off down
the steep bank always
on the outside so as
not to be seen.

They'd jump off by
the old tool factory
rolling head over heels
down the bank crash
landing in snowy willows
cold, battered, but safe.

Walking back to the curve
talking 'bout the great
adventure warmed them to
the task of loading precious
black cargo in a wood hauler
to be divided amongst three
families providing coal enough
for a few more cold
winter nights.

Author's Note: I heard stories like this several times growing up in the Fifties. This one was pulled off in the late Thirties by Pake Lake boys Ed Miller, Charlie Samitis, and my dad Mel. It was risky, illegal as hell, but hey, it was the Depression.

X. Cold Enough To Hang Meat

Heard the stories many times
how cold it was in winter
at the old Park Lake homestead
where north winds blew snow
thru the cracks upstairs
sifting flour-like dustings

over sleeping youngsters.

No wide stairwell here
to let much heat rise
only a square hole to
scramble up to air-cooled
beds heavily layered with
big patchwork quilts.

Leo 'n Mel nailed an
old leather punching bag
to a corner rafter acting
as a fast jabbing
blood warming worker-upper.

Winter mornings started briskly
shaking snow off quilts
leaping union suit long johns
hitting the floor rattling
the punching bag a hard
quick dozen shots seemed
to break the ice nicely.

Stories told of hanging
jack rabbits on nails
partridge by hobble string
venison quarters on hooks
cooling for weeks upstairs
putting meat on the table.

We modern thermostat-controlled
pampered electric blanket pansies
would never hack it
where in the olden days
it was cold enough
to hang meat.

XI. Fast Fling

We met by the bananas
cautiously reaching towards
each other accidentally touching
she gently finger-walking
my arm sending me a
warm fuzzy feeling.

She gave me a sly
look saying she could
walk all over me
leaving me a trembling
mass of uncollected jelly
naming me Smooth Dude
me calling her Tranchie Baby.

But I quickly recoiled
slipping off to the dairy cooler
not wanting her to think
I was one of those
New Wave Supermarket
romance groupies.

Dedicated to the days working at Johnson's Self Serve, where Bill Kibby found a big hairy spider in a banana crate. Yikes!

XII. Dillinger's Raid

Hard times brought boom times
to robbers, kidnappers, murderers
streaking thru Midwest Depression
Halley's Comet with a machine gun
crooks outnumbering carpenters 4   to 1.

Somewhere between Robin Hood
and cold-blooded thug rode John Dillinger.
exhibiting swashbuckling glamor winning
admiration from the downtrodden
leaping over bank teller barriers
taking money from the ones
who'd gotten rich off the poor.

Rumor persisted he once hit
Cadillac around April 1, 1933
robbing the bank escaping
in broad daylight boldly racing
his big black Packard thru town.

Couldn't have been Dillinger
he'd never ride all the way to
Cadillac to rob one bank but
others noted his sister lived
for a while in a little clapboard
cabin south of McBain.

People talked it up for years
how one April morning
three dark-suited men rode
a big black Packard Twin Six
thru Park Lake leaving nothing

but a long trail of rolling dust
and a lot of questions.

Author's Note: There's no record that this happened, but rumors refused to die. It was said Dillinger visited his sister (last house, south end of McBain, east side of the road), ate, and took a nap. Harm Zeeryp swore the big Packard roared past his Park Lake abode scattering chickens and scaring the hogs.

XIII. Leaving New Mexico

Finding New Mexico was easy
turn left at Chicago
blast thru Illinois corn
where big silo groups
serve as skyscrapers then
pass the St. Louis arch
roll and curve thru Missouri
catching showy Branson billboards
past Bass Pro Shop headquarters.

We did Oklahoma living
on Tulsa time one night
then drifted the High Plains
leaving Amarillo in our
rearview mirror gladly heading
South to rugged Apache
country taking refuge in a
frontier saloon displaying
dusty buffalo, muleys, antelope
heads in Carrizozo, New Mexico.

Traffic flowed incessantly oblivious
to time of day going
in opposite directions like

Ron Helmboldt

our two lives interchanging
he switching from student
to college instructor leaving
parents holding a bag
no longer containing a child
but a young man.

Father 'n son found Las Cruces
"City of Crosses" charming
heavily into chile peppers
nut groves alongside Rio Grande
ranches and southwestern decor.

Job at hand focused us
to equip the apartment,
case out the campus and
Astronomy center of NMSU
make things seem more
like a new home than
faceless places far away.

It hit me putting
Cheerios and Corn Chex away
tears welled up dripping
on the stove making
me incredibly sad leaving
me feeling pretty silly.

Early next morning we
left for campus embracing
less like father 'n child
than two men whose
friendship was being separated
by necessity but bittersweet
with regret making it
perfectly all right to cry.

Leaving New Mexico was hard.
Painful lumps crawled up
my chest every exit
heading north causing me
to nearly turn around
at Albuquerque.

Colorado brought some relief
but it was lonely
that night in Canon City,
and heartbreaking for mom
waiting back in Michigan.

I don't even want
to know how hard
it was for him
not for awhile anyway.

Author's Note: Daughter-in-law Stacy says this is my best one ever. I know it was the hardest.

XIV. Roofman Jack

Whap Whap Whap Whap
another shingle down
working way above ground
whap whap whap
another shingle down.

Slap 'em down fast
lap the valley over
bull the chimney well
hear Roofman's yell
owwwww-ooo, owwww-ooo!

Roofman Jack likes shingles
fresh and new but
blasts out tunes mostly
old and blue
his favorite of course
"Up on the Roof" spawns
spirited sing-a-long
rooftop Karaoke.

Up another row
over the top
he has to stop
take the natural high
hear his cry
owwwww-ooo yip yip yip
he be the Roofman.

Cap it off
pop out the jacks
pack up the gun
get out the snacks
gonna have some fun
yip yip yeeha Brewski
Roofman be done!

Dedicated to Jim "Gus Man" Lithen in memory of the fun we've had doing roofs from Grand Rapids to Traverse City. Remember what roofers say: "There's room at the top."

XV. Thunderstruck

She came about midnight
loud, hot, dark, steamy
shaking the very ground
catching me nearly naked
sitting on the back porch.

I played Joe Cool
rocking back and forth
pretending to ignore her advances
her snapping crackling brashness
nonchalantly sipping
Glenmorangie while my
bouncing nervous legs
betrayed near panic.

She just pushed too hard
coming on so heavily
flashing hot tongues of fire
chasing me to the bedroom
trapping me under covers
hoping she wouldn't be
too rough this time.

Could she just leave
her precious gift
and go away?
She indeed departed
during fitful sleep letting
dawn break magnificently
renewing life but
leaving me Thunder Struck.

XVI. North Dakota

Great paired Percherons snorted
stamped dinner plate sized feet
strained at the harness to
till thick sod making way
for wheat, for root crops for
subsistent survival to be
wrenched from the rich soil.

Big Anders plied thick hands
strong back leaning hard
to tame a piece of wild
windy rolling prairie homestead
making a sod house, milk shed
horse barn and granary, orchard
humble nest for wife Liddy
to nurture four little Swedes
who scurried about gathering
faithful gifts from nature
stowing grass twists and
buffalo chips for the stove.

Stuck it out 16 years
through blizzards, drought, locusts
good years and bad 'til
one final crop failure drove
many from the land to
Fargo and a Railroad yard job.

Four generations of human neglect
finds wildness returning reclaiming
niches humans altered but lost
buildings crumbling amid growing
bushes, vines, grasses blanketing

once tamed land now feeding
mice, rabbits, foxes, coyotes, hawks
and that magnificent muley buck
bedding in the orchard.

Nearby smoking noisy diesel
tractors work corporate-owned
fields thousands of acres big
where homesteaders gave all
gallantly wrestling against failure
but now working at the
Bismarck Wal-Mart.

Author's Note: This idea came from a National Geographic before-and-after picture comparing an 1890 farm with its present look. Thousands of small subsistent family farms have disappeared all over America, Marion area included. Corporate giants rule agriculture unless you're Amish. This happened to ancestors of a life-long friend whose great aunt and uncle homesteaded in Dakota, then just disappeared.

XVII. Grand Marais Sunsets

Superior's giant mirror reflects
the last light of day sending
radiant blues, yellows, oranges
sometimes blending mixed clouds
filtering rays uniquely creating
pink to purple color cascades
simply stunning one night
softly subdued the next.

Everyone seems captivated by
ones featuring a giant orange ball
slowly sinking as though
landing on a table top but

sinking right through while
lighting the horizon magnificently
making the big lake seem
a fire.

My favorites come with winged
silhouettes casting black images
mallards, gulls, Canada Geese,
against multi-colored backdrops
often including sound effects as
loons send eerie, mournful cries
out into the night.

Sunsets are to be enjoyed
a reoccurring free show
best seen from the pier
off coast guard point where
fishermen set whitefish ambushes
couples stroll hand in hand
camera buffs click away
don't miss it when visiting
Grand Marais!

XVIII. Hail to the Seasons!

Ten cool things about spring ...
dirty snow piles finally disappearing
brown grass going green
nearly naked baby robins peeping
spindly-legged spotted fawns sunning
kit foxes rolling in clover
morels shouldering through forest debris
berry blossoms blooming beautifully
honking squawking quacking strutting waterfowl

the smell of freshly turned soil
laughing running jumping happy playgrounds.

Ten warm things about summer ...
crackling lightning and rumbling black thunder
the smell of fresh mowed hay
gardens giving golden gifts
moving trails of joggers hikers bikers
sandcastles and bikini beach bunnies
sliding two-run triple at Comerica Park
root beer floats at A&W cruise nite
drilling long drives on pesky par fives
berry pickin' for homemade pie
traveling the highways of America.

Ten fab things about fall ...
crisp air - wilder weather - harvest time
orchards heavy in apples peaches plums
Rocky Mountain Park ringing bull elk bugles
whitetail buck sneaking out for dinner
salmon racing death to spawn upriver
long pass, he has it - TOUCHDOWN!
World Series climaxing to closure
Halloween's ghosts goblins spooky tricksters
Indian corn, pumpkin pie, hot dogs 'n cider
hunting Colorado high country afoot.

Ten VERY COOL things about winter ...
first big snowfall - an Alberta clipper
snowmen snow forts snowball fights
stoking the fireplace to make s'mores
jigging for perch on Portage Lake
cross-country skiers gliding in moonlight
Christmas at Grandma's - kids, presents, food
tying flies listening to Roy Orbison
following high school wrestling to the Palace
sipping apricot brandy in spear shacks

hoping wildlife weather the last storm.

XIX. Amazing Grace

My first look at Amazing Grace
tucked into a Battle Creek
hospital crib revealed a tiny
doll-like sleeping angel giving
ample time to search your
face looking for Mom or Dad
finding neither nor any hair
concluding you were a
perfectly unique creation and
quite Amazing!

You grew up quickly up and out
becoming a truly dazzling
character confounding and capturing
those who touch your life
grabbing your Mom's heart
forever becoming Daddy's girl
leaving grandparents Amazed.

Precious time spent with you
finds a dynamo of energy
flying feet wanting to go fast
busy hands rapidly changing
books by the pile and
monkeys by the arm load
and a host of toys seemingly
ten or so at once
all the while oozing charm
working those snappy eyes
bouncing curls and throwing that

tantalizing smirk to everybody
but occasionally flashing bolts

of hot squealing temper
that can be Amazing too.

Your second year has revealed
Amazing skills of recognition and
attention and ability to quickly
grasp new things making your
grandparents think you're brilliant.

Having you for two years has
been a God-sent thrill to
your grandma giving her new
excitement for shopping and
as for your grandpa
let's put it this way -
I start watching for you
an hour before you arrive
and my heart cries
every time you leave.

XX. Libbus Maximus

In one of my favorite oldies
"Just One Look" Doris Troy sings
"just one look was all it took"
so it was with me in
just one look at you showed
personality oozing charm and at
least a hint of mischievousness too.
You are all of that —
lots of fun, certainly a charmer

's game for about anything.
You're growing up fast
following Big Sister's leads 'n deeds.
And let's not forget to mention –
you're a certified Dancing Crazy!

When you come north
to visit it's busy
riding bikes, playground action
bluegill fishing smacking golf balls
wearing Grandpa out and
shopping with Grandma to give me a break!

After all, one needs rest
to Freddie to "Run Run Rudolph."

PART 5
IN MEMORIAM

Introduction

I chose the following deceased family members and friends for personal reasons. Some of these memorials were recited at their funeral services (Duke Robinson, father-in-law Sid, my dad Mel).

I. Untitled

been thinking about
my ancestors a lot lately
wondering way back
same atoms that composed them
now circle in me

- By my cousin, the poet Terry Wooten. Terry and I often talked about our grandparents and others from the Park Lake era that shaped our make-up and who we are today. We value the heredity.

II. Healer

Great Grandma Mary Helmboldt's
maiden name was Metzger.
The Metzgers came over from Germany,
the southern part
of the Rhine River area,
same time the Helmboldts did.

Mary was a healer
and had gifted hands.
She could stop pain and bleeding.

My dad always told
me stories about her.

Whenever somebody got hurt
in doctorless Park Lake,
people would go get Mary.

Once a cow fell on the ice
and cracked its head.
Its nose wouldn't stop bleeding.
Somebody ran and got Mary.
She placed her hands
on that cow's head,
and said a little prayer or chant,
and the bleeding stopped.

The family was full of stories
like that about her.

III. Six, Eight, Ten, and Two

Such a grueling schedule
four daily stops at the Corner
demanded devotion and persistence beyond
what the common man could muster.

Visiting Marion often included
coffee and breakfast stops at the
Corner where Bud either was
present, just left, or on his way down.

Once we found him there
at quarter to eight causing him
to hastily retreat for home
as we had nearly caught him
in a schedule overlap but
he was back in twenty minutes
freshened for another round.

At first, I laughed and teased
questioning the sanity of four

trips for coffee daily but he
held to his principles as though
civic duty drew him there.

An enjoyable part of visiting Marion
is seeing old friends like Bud
linking us to the hometown
that has a permanent brand
on our very souls.

Six, Eight, Ten, and Two
something only Bud would've conceived
only Bud could've pulled off
only Bud should've been allowed
to do a while longer.

There's an empty chair
no one can fill like
it was filled by ole
Six, Eight, Ten, and Two.

In memory of Bud Crowe

IV. My Buddy Max

Childhood.
Howling wind drifted snow
closed roads and schools
no one would come out
to play 'cept Max.

We stayed out all day
tucked into a big drift
huddled together talking

about being mountain men
trapping the upper Yellowstone
letting snow blow over us
only buddies do that.

High School.
Lost our senior quarterback
lost two straight games
"bring up the kid"
we pleaded to coach.

Max came raw and scared
but guts and pride squelched
nerves as he led us
to four victories in five games
throwing me three TDs
my buddy came through
just like I'd promised.

During college a hard decision
to end the lives of beloved
15-year-old hounds Buck and Shot
required stoutness of heart
we went to Doc Clark
me driving through teary eyes
Max riding in the back
holding both crippled old dogs
telling them they had
earned a long rest
being the best of buddies.

Younger buddies aren't supposed
to go so soon
but he did
they're supposed to be around
for the teasing I need
but he's not

still, he'll always
be my buddy.

V. Don Robinson, Jr.

Don, Butch, Duke
athletic, cocky swagger, sly smirk
child of Don and Elaine
Pontiac Kid with Marion roots.

Robinson, Helmboldt, Lithen
no brothers of their own
hung out together tightly
summer after summer like kin
causing young buck ruckus
making their own fun
building a lifelong bond
creating Duke memories.

Memories like why he's
called Duke the Puke
amazing catches in center field
daring base running antics
dazzling backyard football plays
showing us his best sport -
Dancing! spinning, twisting, finger popping
leaping over our heads
doing the splits pretty
smooth on slow ones too.

Love a strong force in him
loved his family proudly
loved having people stop by
loved being around friends

loved cold beer.

Duke led two lives
before and after the accident
the one that brought
him home to find
himself, family, new friends
interests, knowledge, creativity
capping his life in a
flurry of accomplishment
making things for everybody
things we now have
to remember him by.

VI. Sidney Blaauw

Sid Blaauw
Son of Andrew and Martha
born in Friesland in the Old Country
child of anxiety, excitement, illness, fear
coming to the New World at four years old
brother to Tina, Tillie, Hank, and Gert.

Child of the Great Depression learning
lessons of hard work in hardscrabble times
growing up fast in the 82nd Airborne
grabbing manhood jumping into Nazi turf
earning the Purple Heart then jumping again
into his Dutch homeland for Liberation.

Using a heritage of rollers and blades
he skated into Evelyn Godfrey's heart
his one true love forever fathering
John, Cathy, Sid, and Bob

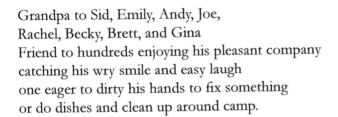

Grandpa to Sid, Emily, Andy, Joe,
Rachel, Becky, Brett, and Gina
Friend to hundreds enjoying his pleasant company
catching his wry smile and easy laugh
one eager to dirty his hands to fix something
or do dishes and clean up around camp.

Loved his family above all
giving them much of his life
leaving them lucky indeed to have
been served by such a dear soul.

Loved his trips to the Jordan
the river running thru his soul
washing away worldly cares
leaving him stalking trout
exactly the utmost in patience.

Loved Western trips to hunt in the mountains
trips to the UP swamps with cherished friends
building great memories rehashed often
revealing he valued the adventure itself
more than bagging a buck.

Later years found him a busy man ·
busy about the house and grounds
busy helping at church, helping his town
making Sparta a community he took pride in
bringing a calm appreciation to the morning
coffee drinkers who understood his role.

The last days were a terrible struggle
frustrating us all, leaving him upset
but he knew his family was there
there to help him find peace
to find eternal rest and salvation
he's watching us now

a very proud man
Sid Blaauw

VII. Mel Helmboldt

Had nicknames -
   Big Mel, Malzone, Melvie, and Gramps
Solid frame, eagle eye, soft hands, strong
Son of Fred and Edna
Park Lake boy of hardscrabble times.
Loved the
   crack of the bat
   tug of a good fish
   thunder of grouse wings
   bobbing antlers of whitetails
   glad voices of visitors
   taste of blended whiskey
   swing music from the Big Bands.
Welcomed
   warm spring rain to spawn morels
   hot summer nights to hatch the caddis
   crisp fall air to signal the hunt
   fresh tracking snow on Sunday morning
   hard ice for jigging bluegills and walleye
   return of spring and Ernie's voice on the radio
   saying "he stood there like the house beside the road."
Performed legendary stuff like
   dropping a six-point from 400 yards on M-66
   bagging two triples on Partridge one Opening Day
   hitting five homers in a Sunday doubleheader
      at Rose Lake ballpark
   catching two 16 inch brookies on back to back casts
   winning three medals at the State Finals in track
   breaking 100 straight skeet targets at the

Marion Rod and Gun Club.
Showed great form
   striking out in the sunshine at Veterans Memorial Park
   blocking the flattest butch or stropping the
     sharpest razor
   flicking a fly under tag alders at Crocker Hole
   running a rack of Eight Ball at Pete's Place
   leaning into a fat whitefish off the Grand Marais pier
   skinning yet another buck in the ole pole barn.
Proud of his family and that his
   wife and children all taught in our schools.
Hated growing old and feeling his skills
   fade like the light of winter.
Remembered for unforgettable Barber Shop stories.
Cheated out of his Golden Years
   by the ravages of dementia,
   body and mind failing him miserably,
   finally taking him to a peaceful rest.
Mel Helmboldt.